AMERICA IN WORDS AND SONG

I Have a Dream

The Story Behind Martin Luther King Jr.'s Most Famous Speech

I HAVE A DREAM
MARTIN LUTHER KING, JR.
THE MARCH ON WASHINGTON
FOR JOBS AND FREEDOM
AUGUST 28, 1963

CHELSEA
CLUBHOUSE
An Imprint of Chelsea House Publishers

Kerry A. Graves

I Have a Dream

Copyright © 2004 by Infobase Publishing

Chelsea House
An imprint of Infobase Publishing
132 West 31st Street
New York NY 10001

Printed and bound in the United States of America.

9 8 7 6 5 4 3 2

Library of Congress Cataloging-in-Publication Data
Graves, Kerry A.
  I have a dream : the story behind Martin Luther King Jr.'s most famous speech / by Kerry A. Graves.
        p. cm. — (America in words and song)
Summary: Explains the meaning and historical context of Martin Luther King Jr.'s "I Have a Dream" speech, also providing biographical information about Dr. King and discussing the Civil Rights Movement.
Includes bibliographical references and index.
  ISBN 0-7910-7335-1
  1. King, Martin Luther, Jr., 1929-1968. I have a dream—Juvenile literature. 2. King, Martin Luther, Jr., 1929-1968—Oratory—Juvenile literature. 3. March on Washington for Jobs and Freedom, Washington, D.C., 1963—Juvenile literature. 4. Speeches, addresses, etc., American—Washington (D.C.)—Juvenile literature. 5. African Americans—Civil rights—History—20th century— Juvenile literature. 6. Civil rights movements—United States— History—20th century—Juvenile literature.
[1. King, Martin Luther, Jr., 1929-1968. 2. March on Washington for Jobs and Freedom, Washington, D.C., 1963. 3. African Americans— Civil rights. 4. Civil rights movements.] I. Title. II. Series.
E185.97.K5G73 2004
323'.092—dc21   2003004042

Selected Sources

Hansen, Drew D. *The Dream: Martin Luther King, Jr. and the Speech that Inspired a Nation*. New York: Ecco, 2003.

King, Martin Luther, Jr. *The Autobiography of Martin Luther King, Jr.* Edited by Clayborne Carson. New York: Intellectual Properties Management in association with Warner Books, 1998.

The Martin Luther King, Jr. Papers Project at Stanford University
www.stanford.edu/group/King

U.S. Department of State International Information Programs: March on Washington
usinfo.state.gov/usa/civilrights/anniversary

Editorial Credits

Lois Wallentine, editor; Takeshi Takahashi, designer; Mary Englar, photo researcher; Jennifer Krassy Peiler, layout

Content reviewer:

Melissa English-Rias, Chief of Interpretation and Education, Martin Luther King Jr. National Historic Site, Atlanta, Ga

Photo Credits

AP/Wide World: cover, 4, 5, 8, 17, 22, 25, 30; ©Reuters NewMedia Inc./CORBIS: title page, 20; ©Flip Schulke/CORBIS: 4, 6, 13, 16, 23; ©Bettmann/CORBIS: 7, 9, 10, 11, 14, 15, 18, 24, 27; Library of Congress: 12; Paul Schutzer/Time Life Pictures/Getty Images: 19; Dan Budnik/Woodfin Camp/Time Life Pictures/Getty Images: 26.

Table of Contents

Introduction

Nearly 250,000 people crowded around the Lincoln Memorial and the reflecting pool to hear civil rights speakers at the 1963 event.

Martin Luther King Jr. delivers his "I Have a Dream" speech at the March on Washington for Jobs and Freedom.

On August 28, 1963, Martin Luther King Jr. stood on the steps of the Lincoln Memorial in Washington, D.C. He looked over the hot, tired crowd. Nearly 250,000 people had come together for the March on Washington for Jobs and Freedom. That morning, black people and white people had walked together through the city's streets. Afterward, they gathered in front of the memorial to listen to songs and speeches from **civil rights** leaders.

The marchers were protesting the unfair treatment of black people. **Discrimination** against blacks occurred across the nation. Many hotels, restaurants, and businesses refused to serve them. Blacks did not have the same opportunities for education, housing, or jobs that whites did. The **segregated** South, where blacks were kept apart from whites, was full of violence and hatred. In many areas, blacks were not allowed to vote, and they did not receive equal treatment under the law.

Four-year-old Andrew Franklin White-Cleary sits on the landing of the Lincoln Memorial in the exact spot where Martin Luther King Jr. delivered his "I Have a Dream" speech. In 2003, the words were carved into the granite steps to serve as a memorial to the event.

King was the last speaker of the day. He talked about the struggles and injustices black people endured. Near the end of his written speech, he looked up from his notes and started to speak from his heart. "Even though we face the difficulties of today and tomorrow, I still have a dream," he said. "It is a dream deeply rooted in the American dream." King shared his vision of a world where race wouldn't matter, where all people lived together peacefully and enjoyed the same rights. Thousands of voices cheered and called out "keep dreamin'," "I see it," and "dream on!"

In 1963, Dr. King's moving words brought people together and helped to change the country's laws. Even today, the speech still motivates people around the world to work for equality, freedom, and justice. In fact, his message remains so powerful that in 2003, on the 40th anniversary of the March on Washington, the words "I Have a Dream" were carved in the steps of the Lincoln Memorial. The words mark the exact place where King stood to deliver his speech. It is a spot some have called "sacred ground."

Martin Luther King Jr.

On January 15, 1929, there was great excitement at 501 Auburn Avenue in Atlanta, Georgia. Mrs. Alberta Williams King gave birth to a son. He was named Martin Luther King Jr. after his father. Martin grew up with his older sister and younger brother in the neighborhood known as Sweet Auburn, where many middle-income black families lived.

In the South, blacks faced **prejudice** daily, but Martin's parents worked hard to teach their children self-respect. Martin's mother explained that even though the South used segregation laws to keep the races separate, blacks should never feel **inferior**. "You are as good as anyone," she told Martin. Martin's father, Reverend Martin Luther King Sr., also provided a good example for his children. As a strong supporter of equal rights, he refused to ride segregated city buses. He wouldn't shop at businesses that only served blacks in the back of the store.

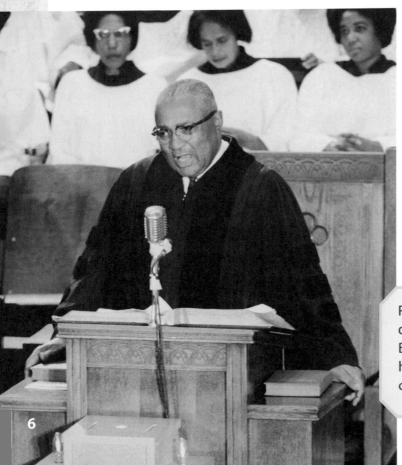

Reverend Martin Luther King Sr. delivers a sermon at Ebenezer Baptist Church in Atlanta. He taught his children and members of the congregation about self-worth.

Segregation practices were sometimes called Jim Crow laws. "Jim Crow" was the name of a black character in an 1830s song. At first, "Jim Crow" was used to describe the **stereotyped** image of all blacks. By the 1880s, the term also referred to the laws, practices, and organizations that supported segregation.

Throughout the South, Jim Crow laws kept blacks and whites segregated in public places. Blacks had to use "colored only" waiting rooms, rest rooms, and water fountains. They could only sit in the back of city buses, and they had to give up their seats if white passengers needed them. Stores, restaurants, movie theaters, and hotels often had separate entrances and seating areas for blacks, if they served blacks at all. Blacks and whites lived in separate neighborhoods and attended separate schools. In many places, blacks could not vote.

Jim Crow laws endured for more than 80 years. Finally, in the 1950s and 1960s, the Supreme Court ruled against segregation in several cases. Congress awarded blacks new protection under the Civil Rights Acts of 1964 and 1968. The civil rights movement led by Martin Luther King Jr. helped to bring many Jim Crow practices to an end.

Jim Crow laws forced black people to use separate waiting rooms at bus and train stations.

"I could never adjust to the separate waiting rooms, separate eating places, separate rest rooms, partly because the separate was always unequal, and partly because the very idea of separation did something to my sense of dignity and self-respect."

—Martin Luther King Jr.

Martin Luther King Jr. learned about prejudice and discrimination through childhood experiences. As an adult, he made it his mission to work for change.

Martin's first personal experience with **racism** happened when he was about 6 years old. A white friend told him that his father wouldn't let them play together anymore. Martin's parents explained that some people were prejudiced against blacks, but they told him not to hate whites because of it. As a young boy, Martin had a hard time understanding this.

In high school, Martin started speaking out about segregation and problems in the South. When he was 14 years old, he won a contest with a speech titled "The Negro and the Constitution." He said the nation would be more successful if everyone had "fair play and free opportunity." Yet, on his bus ride home from Dublin, Georgia, to Atlanta, he faced segregation again. Martin and his teacher had to give their seats to white passengers and stand for the entire 90-mile (145-kilometer) trip.

When he was 15 years old, Martin started college in Atlanta. After graduating, he continued his education at a school in Chester, Pennsylvania. He earned a degree to be a minister. Next, he studied for an advanced degree at Boston University. Martin met Coretta Scott during his time in Boston. On their first date, Martin told her that they should get married. Coretta, who wanted to become a concert singer, was doubtful. Yet, less than 18 months later, on June 18, 1953, they became husband and wife.

Martin believed he could best fight discrimination through the church. In 1954, he became the pastor of the Dexter Avenue Baptist Church in Montgomery, Alabama. He always encouraged his congregation to discuss the racist conditions around them. He set up a social and political action committee, and he made sure everyone was registered to vote in elections. His influence on civil rights issues had begun.

Throughout their marriage, Coretta Scott King joined her husband in working for civil rights.

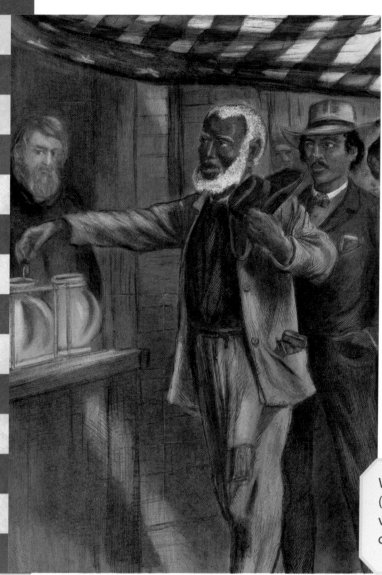

Black people have been struggling for centuries to gain equality in America. They fought against their status as slaves from the late 1600s until President Abraham Lincoln signed the Emancipation Proclamation in 1863. Soon after, slaves were freed and given the rights of citizens through the 13th and 14th Amendments to the Constitution.

But by the late 1800s, prejudiced white Southerners passed state laws that went against the new amendments. These laws supported segregation practices and kept blacks from voting. Violent hate groups also erupted across the South. Black people were threatened, beaten, murdered, and had crosses burned in their yards.

When slaves became citizens after the Civil War (1861–1865), black men earned the right to vote. But Southern whites soon passed "black codes" that took this and other rights away.

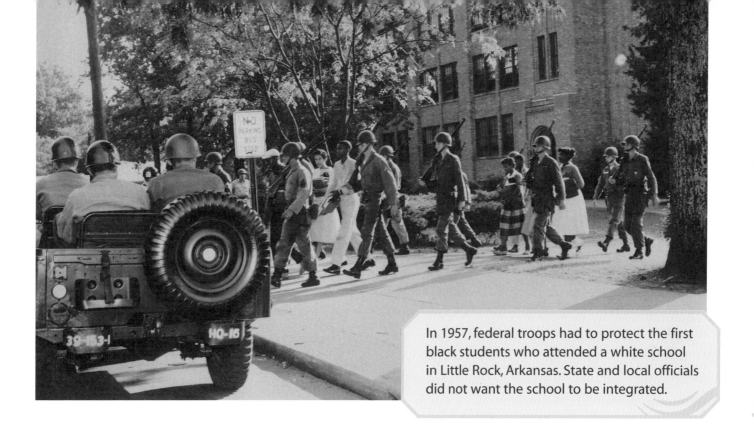

In 1957, federal troops had to protect the first black students who attended a white school in Little Rock, Arkansas. State and local officials did not want the school to be integrated.

In 1909, a group of 60 black and white leaders formed the National Association for the Advancement of Colored People (NAACP). This organization worked to protect blacks from violence, unfair treatment under the law, and discrimination. In the 1950s, the NAACP supported a lawsuit against segregated schools in Topeka, Kansas. The Supreme Court finally settled this case, called *Brown* v. *Board of Education*, in 1954. The court said designating separate schools for blacks was unconstitutional. Even so, many Southern schools failed to **integrate**, or admit students of both races, for years.

Rosa Parks and the Montgomery Bus Boycott

On December 1, 1955, Rosa Parks boarded a city bus and sat down in one of the rear seats assigned to blacks. The driver ordered Parks and other black passengers to stand so whites could sit. The other passengers moved, but Parks refused. Police officers arrested her.

In response, the black community in Montgomery refused to ride buses until segregation laws were lifted. Blacks walked, carpooled, or took cabs to work. Without the black riders, the bus company lost money. City officials were angry. Police officers arrested people on minor charges to scare them into breaking the boycott. The city took Martin Luther King Jr. and others to court, saying that the boycott was against an old Alabama law. A judge ruled against King, but he **appealed**, calling on a higher court to examine the case. Finally, the U.S. Supreme Court ruled that Alabama's state and local bus segregation laws were illegal. On December 21, 1956, blacks in Montgomery rode desegregated buses for the first time.

For many blacks, fighting discrimination through the courts took too long. They decided to take direct action against racist laws or situations. One successful example was the Montgomery Bus **Boycott** in 1955. During this protest, thousands of black people refused to ride on the segregated city buses. Black community leaders elected Martin Luther King Jr. to lead the boycott. King asked protestors to remain peaceful, even if they were arrested or mistreated. Their nonviolent boycott worked. After 382 days, blacks in Montgomery earned the right to sit anywhere they wanted on city buses. They also did not have to give up their seats to white passengers.

A police officer takes Rosa Parks's fingerprints. She started the Montgomery Bus Boycott with her refusal to obey segregation codes.

Martin Luther King Jr. learned about peaceful protest methods through many sources. He read about nonviolent resistance, which means refusing to cooperate with a system that is unjust. But King's greatest influence was Mohandas Gandhi. Gandhi was a native of the country of India, which had been controlled by Great Britain since the 1700s. Many laws discriminated against the Indian people. Gandhi led his people to peacefully disobey the unfair laws. His movement brought about India's independence from Great Britain in 1947.

King felt the nonviolent methods that Gandhi used would help in the civil rights movement. Like Gandhi, King began to organize marches, boycotts, and **sit-ins**. Above all, he told protesters to remain peaceful and not to resist arrest or fight back if they were attacked. King believed the "weapon of love" would be powerful. "We must have compassion and understanding for those who hate us," he said.

"I believe that it is impossible to end hatred with hatred."

—Mohandas Gandhi

The King family prays before eating dinner. A portrait of Mohandas Gandhi hangs above the doorway. Gandhi's peaceful protest methods inspired Martin.

In 1960, four black college students in Greensboro, North Carolina, began a sit-in at a "whites-only" lunch counter. They politely asked for service, but no one would wait on them.

In 1957, King and more than 100 black leaders formed the Southern Christian Leadership Conference (SCLC). The purpose of the group was to organize nonviolent protest efforts. The leaders unanimously elected King as the SCLC's president.

King began speaking across the country to promote civil rights for blacks. This kept him from his job at the Dexter Avenue Baptist Church. In 1960, he decided to move to Atlanta to be near SCLC headquarters. He also became a copastor at Ebenezer Baptist Church in Atlanta, where his father was senior pastor.

King's peaceful protest methods caught on. In the 1960s, thousands of civil rights **activists** began holding sit-ins at "whites-only" lunch counters. During boycotts, blacks refused to shop at segregated businesses. "Freedom Rides," where black and white activists rode buses across the country to test segregation rules, started in 1961. Black passengers refused to move to the back of the bus when they arrived in Southern states. And people held marches across the country to call attention to civil rights issues.

While protesters remained peaceful, they often met violence from others. During the Montgomery Bus Boycott, black homes and churches were bombed. At sit-ins, activists were threatened and sometimes arrested. In 1961, angry white Southerners set one of the Freedom Riders' buses on fire and attacked riders on another. In Alabama in 1963, the Birmingham police force used clubs, fire hoses, and dogs against thousands of marchers. Still the activists did not answer violence with any violence.

Some white people thought blacks should wait for the government to act instead of holding protests. In 1963, King wrote his "Letter from a Birmingham Jail." He explained why blacks could no longer wait for equal rights:

"When you have seen vicious mobs lynch [kill] your mothers and fathers at will…when you have seen hate-filled policemen curse, kick, and even kill your black brothers and sisters…when you are humiliated day in and day out by nagging signs reading 'white' and 'colored'…when

Freedom Riders watch as smoke rolls out the door of their Greyhound bus. A mob of white people, angry over the Freedom Riders' attempt to break segregation rules, slashed the tires and set the bus on fire.

you are forever fighting a degenerating sense of 'nobodiness'—then you will understand why we find it difficult to wait."

The extreme violence in Birmingham led President John F. Kennedy to send a new civil rights bill to Congress. King and other leaders began organizing a march in Washington, D.C. They hoped to pressure politicians to pass President Kennedy's bill.

The March on Washington

Leaders for the March on Washington for Jobs and Freedom had only two months to prepare. They wanted to hold a fully integrated protest, with at least 100,000 black and white marchers. Bayard Rustin, who worked as an aide to Martin Luther King Jr., organized the plans for this huge demonstration. He and his staff advertised the event, arranged for the marchers' transportation, set up the march route and meeting places in Washington, D.C., and scheduled the program. Across the country, people handed out manuals describing how to reach Washington, D.C., and where to go.

Marchers traveled to the nation's capital on more than 40 special trains, 2,200 chartered buses, and thousands of private cars. Those who could afford airfare boarded planes. A group from Brooklyn, New York, walked 237 miles (382 kilometers) to the event. On August 28, 1963, people of all ages, all religions, and all backgrounds headed for Washington, D.C.

Early in the morning, a group of protesters make their way to the meeting point for the March on Washington for Jobs and Freedom. People from communities across the United States took part in the march on August 28, 1963.

Civil rights leaders had planned to march on Washington, D.C., before 1963. In 1941, labor union leader A. Philip Randolph had planned to hold a march with 100,000 protesters. He wanted to call attention to the lack of jobs for blacks. However, 10 days before the march, President Franklin D. Roosevelt gave an executive order to defense manufacturers with government contracts. The order said these factories could not discriminate against blacks. Randolph called off the march.

In June 1963, six civil rights leaders, including Randolph, met with President John F. Kennedy. They told him they planned to carry out a mass demonstration in Washington, D.C. Kennedy had just introduced a bill to Congress that, among other measures, outlawed discrimination in public places. His bill would eliminate many Jim Crow laws. Kennedy believed a march at this time would anger members of Congress. He feared the bill would not pass.

Randolph, King, and the other leaders insisted the march was necessary to achieve their purpose. Kennedy ended the meeting by agreeing not to speak out against the march. But the president still worried that either violence would erupt or marchers would be too few in number to make an impact.

"[The march] will have a two-fold purpose…to arouse the conscience of the nation on the economic plight of the Negro…and to demand strong forthright civil rights legislation."

—Martin Luther King Jr.

Six civil rights leaders formed the core committee for the March on Washington for Jobs and Freedom. They are, from left to right: John Lewis, Whitney Young, A. Philip Randolph, Martin Luther King Jr., James Farmer, and Roy Wilkins.

Martin Luther King Jr. and other leaders link arms or hold hands as they march down Constitution Avenue. Protesters behind them carry signs demanding civil rights.

The day was filled with anticipation. Marchers started gathering at dawn near the Washington Monument. By 9:30 in the morning, fewer than 25,000 people had shown up. But the crowd steadily grew. They listened to musical performances and speeches from celebrities. By 11 A.M., at least 90,000 people had arrived, and many more were on the way.

The area around the monument was extremely crowded. Without being directed, some protesters began marching toward the Lincoln Memorial. King and the other

planners hurried to join the group heading down Constitution Avenue. More marchers walked down Independence Avenue.

People were emotional, yet relaxed and peaceful. Many marchers carried signs with **slogans** demanding civil rights. Some sang protest songs such as "We Shall Overcome." There was no violence from the protesters. The three arrests police made that day were of people acting out against the march. The officers and armed troops on hand directed traffic and helped marchers who suffered from the heat.

At the Lincoln Memorial, the first marchers filled up the steps. More and more people crowded around the front of the reflecting pool. By 1 P.M., nearly 250,000 marchers had gathered, making it the largest group in history to ever assemble on the Mall. Some people stood more than half a mile away from the memorial. They couldn't hear the people on stage, so they turned on their radios to listen to the remarks by civil rights and religious leaders and to enjoy the music.

However, most of the speeches and performances didn't have much of an impact on the crowd. Standing under the hot sun, people grew restless. Some marchers left, while others napped under trees. Then 23-year-old John Lewis, leader of a national civil rights group for students, stirred up the audience. In his speech, he reminded the crowd of the struggles black people faced and why they were marching. "By the force of our demands, our determination, and our numbers," he declared, "we shall splinter the segregated South into a thousand pieces and put them together in the image of God and democracy." People cheered his call to "Wake up, America," and pass strong civil rights laws.

A bit later, gospel singer Mahalia Jackson sang a slave spiritual that brought tears to the eyes of the marchers. Finally Martin Luther King Jr. stepped forward to deliver the closing speech.

A quarter of a million people gathered to listen to the afternoon program at the Lincoln Memorial. The crowd appears to stretch all the way back to the Washington Monument, where the march started.

19

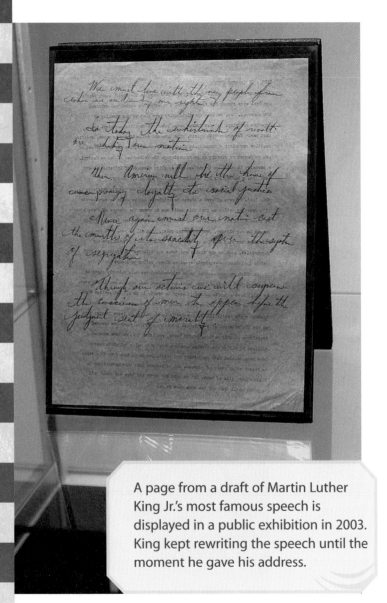

A page from a draft of Martin Luther King Jr.'s most famous speech is displayed in a public exhibition in 2003. King kept rewriting the speech until the moment he gave his address.

Four days before the march, Martin Luther King Jr. started working on his speech. A few of his aides had prepared rough drafts, to which other civil rights leaders added their ideas. King not only wanted the perfect content, but he also wanted exactly the right rhythm for his words. He kept writing and revising. He gave the speech to his typist about 4 A.M. on August 28, but he made additional notes on the typed copy later that day.

King had already delivered more than 350 speeches that year. He had memorized many passages, and he reused them as he needed when he wanted to make a certain point. Normally people didn't help him to write his speeches, nor did he spend this much time preparing. But this speech was different. The whole world was watching.

Standing on the steps of the Lincoln Memorial that afternoon, King first reminded the marchers that President Lincoln had signed the Emancipation Proclamation 100 years earlier, yet blacks were still not free. Segregation, discrimination, and poverty were the "chains" holding them back.

King quoted the Declaration of Independence, which guaranteed all men the "rights of Life, Liberty, and the pursuit of Happiness." These rights are owed to blacks, he stated, and the government promised to pay. But America had written a "bad check" for blacks, one "marked **'insufficient** funds.'" King vowed they would still cash that check.

King urged America to stop racial discrimination and end the unfair treatment of blacks. He cautioned that the march was not an end to the efforts for freedom, but a beginning. He instructed protesters to remain dignified and calm while working for a better life. They shouldn't let hatred or bitterness bring violence into their protests.

He stressed that whites and blacks must work together for freedom, because all our lives are tied together.

King then advised the marchers to return to their homes and continue to struggle for equality. He encouraged everyone not to lose hope and promised they would succeed.

"On that glorious day in August 1963, I felt as if the spirit of history was guiding our steps....We came to petition our government for change. We came to demonstrate the sense of urgency. We wanted the federal government...to see, hear, and feel the pain, struggle, and determination of the indigenous [native] people of the segregated South and ghettos of the North."

—Congressman John Lewis, speaking at the 40th anniversary of the March on Washington, August 2003

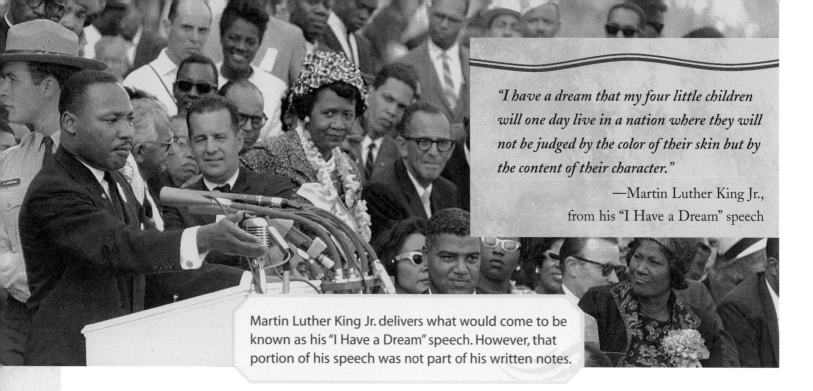

"I have a dream that my four little children will one day live in a nation where they will not be judged by the color of their skin but by the content of their character."

—Martin Luther King Jr., from his "I Have a Dream" speech

Martin Luther King Jr. delivers what would come to be known as his "I Have a Dream" speech. However, that portion of his speech was not part of his written notes.

At that moment, King paused. Sitting near the podium, Mahalia Jackson is believed to have said, "Tell them about the dream, Martin!" Later, King said the positive reaction of the crowd brought to mind the phrase, "I have a dream," which he had used in other speeches.

The tone of King's voice began to change. He began to use the voice of a preacher. He stopped reading from his written notes and began to speak from his heart: "I say to you today, my friends: so even though we face the difficulties of today and tomorrow, I still have a dream. It is a dream deeply rooted in the American dream."

King would repeat the phrase "I have a dream," eight more times. Nearly every time he described a scene, including:

★ Citizens across the nation living out the promise of equality found in the Declaration of Independence.

★ The children of slaves and children of slave owners becoming friends.

★ Peace and justice taking hold, even in the state of Mississippi, where racial hatred and violence ran strong.

★ His children being measured by the "content of their character" instead of "the color of their skin."

★ Black children and white children all holding hands "as sisters and brothers."

King told the marchers to bring these hopes back to their homes and continue to work for civil rights. He called their attention to the first verse of the song, "My Country 'Tis of Thee," and repeated the last line, "let freedom ring," again and again. He asked for the bells of freedom to ring out from all parts of the country. He named mountains in the east and west, then places in the segregated South, including "every hill and molehill of Mississippi."

Then, with the audience hanging on his every word, King brought the speech to a close:

"And when this happens, when we allow freedom to ring, when we let it ring from every village and every hamlet, from every state and every city, we will be able to speed up that day when all of God's children, black men and white men, Jews and Gentiles, Protestants and Catholics, will be able to join hands and sing in the words of the old Negro spiritual, 'Free at last, free at last. Thank God Almighty, we are free at last.'"

The crowd erupted in cheers and applause. It was an emotional and positive ending to the day. Slowly, protesters headed back to the trains, cars, buses, and planes that had brought them.

Listeners cheer after hearing King's speech of hope and inspiration at the March on Washington for Jobs and Freedom.

23

After the Speech

The March on Washington impressed many Americans. However, it also angered Southerners who were opposed to integration. On September 15, 1963, a bomb exploded at a black Baptist church in Birmingham. Four teenage girls were killed and 21 other children were injured by the explosion. Two months later, on November 22, President Kennedy was murdered. The entire nation was stunned. Leaders wondered what would happen to the civil rights bill in Congress.

The new president, Lyndon B. Johnson, did support civil rights. In 1964, he signed the Civil Rights Act ending segregation in schools, libraries, and playgrounds. It banned discrimination in hiring practices and in hotels and motels.

President Lyndon Johnson hands Martin Luther King Jr. the pen he used to sign the Civil Rights Act of 1964 into law.

Martin Luther King Jr. and his wife Coretta lead protesters for voting rights on a five-day march from Selma, Alabama, to the state capital grounds in Montgomery.

In December 1964, King won the Nobel Peace Prize, which recognized his hard work and peaceful methods in fighting for equality for blacks. People all over the world celebrated this proud moment. This motivated civil rights activists to continue with their struggle.

On March 7, 1965, protesters started a march from Selma, Alabama, to the state capital in Montgomery. They wanted to make it known that blacks were still being denied voting rights. At the very start of the march armed state police officers attacked protesters with clubs and tear gas, injuring hundreds. The day became known as Bloody Sunday. The national media attention drew thousands of additional marchers when the event was rescheduled. King led the second march and spoke at the state capitol. He told the crowd, "I know you are asking today, 'How long will it [justice] take?'…Not long, because no lie can live forever."

Five months later, President Johnson signed the Voting Rights Act of 1965 into law. This act eliminated the discriminating tactics used to keep blacks from voting.

> *"We have been repeatedly faced with the cruel irony of watching Negro and white boys...kill and die together for a nation that has been unable to seat them together in the same schools."*
>
> —Martin Luther King Jr.

In the late 1960s, King became concerned with the state of the civil rights movement. He felt the new Black Power groups promoted hatred and violence.

As riots occurred over the next few years in cities across the country, King became increasingly concerned with racial violence. He wanted to focus attention on improving education for blacks so they could find better jobs to lead them out of poverty. He also opposed the Vietnam War (1954–1975), saying that black soldiers were being sent to fight for the rights of people in South Vietnam, but, "...the black American soldier has himself never experienced democracy."

In 1968, King traveled to a Memphis, Tennessee, protest for black sanitation workers who were demanding better wages. On April 3, he spoke at a rally. He wondered about his own death, saying:

> "Like anybody, I would like to live a long life.... But I'm not concerned about that now. I just want to do God's will. And He's allowed me to go up to the mountain. And I've looked over, and I've seen the promised land. I may not get there with you. But I want you to know tonight, that we, as a people, will get to the promised land."

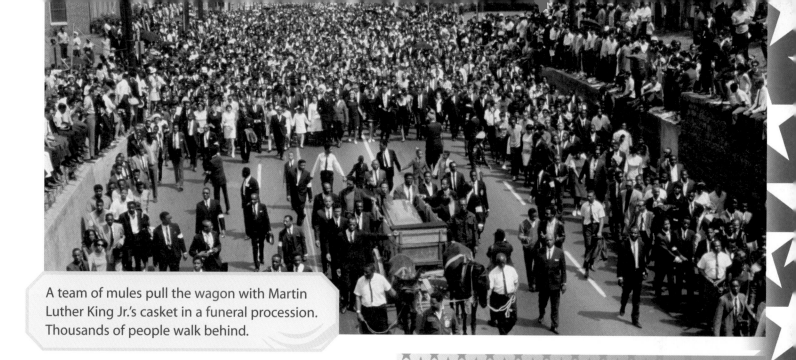

A team of mules pull the wagon with Martin Luther King Jr.'s casket in a funeral procession. Thousands of people walk behind.

The next night, King was shot on the balcony of the Lorraine Motel in Memphis. He died in surgery a short time later. At his funeral in Atlanta on April 9, the church held only 800 mourners, but between 60,000 to 100,000 others listened to the service outdoors on loudspeakers. His hearse was a farm cart drawn by two mules, and 50,000 people followed the casket to the cemetery in King's last march. His marble tombstone is engraved with the slave spiritual phrase: "Free at Last, Free at Last, Thank God Almighty, I'm Free at Last."

Blacks in the United States Today

The struggle for equality continues for blacks in America. Efforts to make society aware of black culture resulted in better black history materials in schools, more black characters in movies and television, and the popularity of black authors and their novels. Successful black athletes and entertainers have become role models for black youth. However, problems such as single-parent households, gang violence, poor education systems, lack of skilled jobs, and unemployment all need to be addressed in the 21st century.

December 1955

On December 1, Rosa Parks refuses to give her bus seat to a white passenger. Four days later, King leads black people in the Montgomery Bus Boycott.

November 1956

The U.S. Supreme Court rules that bus segregation is unconstitutional. The Montgomery Bus Boycott ends December 21.

May 1961

White and black students organize Freedom Rides to protest segregated interstate buses.

1954

The U.S. Supreme Court rules that public schools must be desegregated in their decision for *Brown* v. *Board of Education* of Topeka (Kansas).

October 1954

King officially becomes the pastor at Dexter Avenue Baptist Church in Montgomery, Alabama.

1929

On January 15, 1929 Martin Luther King Jr. is born in Atlanta, Georgia.

1929

1950

1960

Summer, 1963

President John F. Kennedy introduces a new civil rights bill. The March on Washington for Jobs and Freedom where King delivers his "I Have a Dream" speech is held.

February 1960

Sit-in protests begin at segregated food service lunch counters in Greensboro, North Carolina.

Fall 1963

In September, the bombing of the Sixteenth Avenue Baptist Church kills four girls. In November, President Kennedy is assassinated.

July 1964

President Johnson signs the Civil Rights Act of 1964 into law.

March 7, 1965

In Alabama, police attack protesters marching from Selma to Montgomery; King leads a successful march two weeks later.

August 1965

President Johnson signs the Voting Rights Act into law; this outlaws literacy tests.

January 1968

Civil Rights Act of 1968 becomes law, which makes discrimination in selling, renting, or financing homes illegal.

April 1968

King travels to Memphis, Tennessee, to support striking sanitation workers. On April 4, King is assassinated at the Lorraine Motel. His funeral is held in Atlanta, Georgia, on April 9.

1965   *1970*

Historical Highlights of the 1950s and 1960s

While the fight for Civil Rights was taking place, what else was happening in the world?

★ The January 1, 1954, *Rose Parade* is the first television program to be broadcast country-wide in color.

★ In 1954, Elvis Presley signs a recording contract and becomes one of the most popular singers in America.

★ Fidel Castro takes power in Cuba after the Cuban Revolution of 1959.

★ In 1959, Alaska and Hawaii become the 49th and 50th states of the United States of America.

★ In 1961, Alan Shepard becomes the first U.S. astronaut to go to space.

★ The Beatles are first introduced to U.S. fans in 1964 on the *Ed Sullivan Show*.

★ President Lyndon B. Johnson sends first U.S. ground combat troops to the Vietnam War in 1965 (war ends in 1975).

★ Dr. Christiaan N. Barnard and his group of South African surgeons perform the first human heart transplant in 1967. Their patient lives 18 days.

★ Astronauts Neil Armstrong and Buzz Aldrin take the first walk on the moon in 1969.

activist (AK-ti-vist) a person who takes part in a movement to change rules or people's minds

appeal (uh-PEEL) to ask a higher court to examine a ruling from a lower court to see if it should be changed

Coretta Scott King and three of her children visit the memorial to her husband's "I Have a Dream" speech on the 40th anniversary of the March on Washington in 2003.

boycott (BOI-kot) to refuse to buy something or take part in something as a way of making a protest

civil rights (SIV-il RITES) the rights that all people in a society have; civil rights are protected by law; some civil rights in the United States are the right to own property, the right to equal treatment under the law, and the right to vote

discriminate (diss-KRIM-uh-nate) to treat other people unfairly because of prejudice

inferior (in-FIHR-ee-ur) not as good as something or someone else

insufficient (in-suh-FISH-uhnt) not enough

integrate (IN-tuh-grate) to include people of all races

prejudice (PREJ-uh-diss) hatred or unfair treatment that results from having an unfair opinion about a group of people based on their race, religion, or other characteristic

racism (RAY-siz-uhm) the belief that people of one race are better than people of another race

segregate (SEG-ruh-gate) to separate or keep people or things apart from the main group

sit-in (SIT-in) a demonstration where protesters sit in chairs or on the floor and refuse to leave a business or site until their demands are met

slogan (SLOH-guhn) a phrase that expresses an idea, goal, or belief

stereotype (STER-ee-oh-tipe) an overly simple opinion of a person or group

To Learn More

READ THESE BOOKS

Clayborne, Anna. *Gandhi: The Peaceful Revolutionary*. Austin, Texas: Raintree Steck-Vaughn, 2003.

Haskins, James. *The March on Washington*. New York: Harper Collins, 1993.

_____. *I Have a Dream: The Life and Words of Martin Luther King Jr.* Brookfield, Conn.: Millbrook Press, 1992.

King, Casey and Linda Barrett Osborne. *Oh, Freedom!: Kids Talk about the Civil Rights Movement with the People Who Made It Happen*. Foreword by Rosa Parks. New York: A.A. Knopf, 1997.

Santella, Andrew. *Martin Luther King Jr.: Civil Rights Leader and Nobel Prize Winner*. Chanhassen, Minn.: Child's World, 2004.

Summer, L. S. *The March on Washington*. Chanhassen, Minn.: Child's World, 2001.

Turck, Mary. *The Civil Rights Movement for Kids: A History with 21 Activities*. Chicago: Chicago Review Press, 2000.

Venable, Rose. *The Civil Rights Movement*. Chanhassen, Minn.: Child's World, 2002.

LOOK UP THESE INTERNET SITES

Civil Rights in the United States

usinfo.state.gov/usa/civilrights/homepage.htm
Review current information about civil rights efforts in America.

LIFE Magazine: Martin Luther King Jr. Classic Images

www.life.com/Life/mlk/mlkpics.html
View a collection of photographs of Martin Luther King Jr. from past issues of *Life* magazine.

The Life of Martin Luther King Jr.

www.stanford.edu/group/King/
Click on the Popular Requests link and hear clips from the "I Have a Dream" speach or explore the interactive chronology.

National Public Radio: March on Washington Anniversary

www.npr.org/news/specials/march40th/index.html
Follow NPR's coverage on the 40th anniversary of the March on Washington for Jobs and Freedom.

National Register of Historic Places: March on Washington

www.cr.nps.gov/NR/feature/marchonwash/marchonwashington.htm
Follow links to many historic places that played a role in the civil rights movement in America.

seattletimes.com: Martin Luther King Jr.

seattletimes.nwsource.com/mlk/king
Learn more about King's role in the civil rights movement.

INTERNET SEARCH KEY WORDS:

Martin Luther King Jr., "I Have a Dream," March on Washington for Jobs and Freedom, civil rights movement